E. J. H.

Bible Scenes

E. J. H.

Bible Scenes

ISBN/EAN: 9783337171759

Printed in Europe, USA, Canada, Australia, Japan

Cover: Foto ©Lupo / pixelio.de

More available books at **www.hansebooks.com**

BIBLE SCENES.

WITH ILLUSTRATIONS.

NEW YORK:
ANSON D. F. RANDOLPH & COMPANY,

BIBLE SCENE, No. 1.—OLD AND NEW.

A NARROW valley, or deep cleft through a beautifully wooded country; a swift river, that rushes over its rocky bed, on to the sea; trees of foreign growth along its banks, closed in on each side by high hills clothed with verdure.

Coming up the valley, returning to his home, a traveller is seen, a kingly man in costly dress, but rent and stained as if in recent strife. Lost in thought he moves slowly on, until arriving at the river's ford he stops, and seems as if gazing down the coming years. Suddenly a man in Priestly robes stands before him. He looks like one in whom is lodged the very power and wisdom of Jehovah, yet a man bound by closest ties to every other man. In his hands are the mystic emblems—bread and wine. Now the hands are raised in blessing, as the traveller bows in homage and offers gifts.

A thousand years are past, and the name appears in Messianic Psalm. Again a thousand years, and beside that rapid river, a great crowd has gathered. Tall reeds, rocks and sand, and wild stony hills have changed the valley to a wilderness. All ranks are there—priest and peasant—soldiers with helmet and sword, mothers with infants, sailors from distant ports, wild Arabs, shepherds and traders—all attent, gazing upon a

tall, slight man, with face bronzed by sun and wind, his long
shaggy hair—uncut from childhood; over his shoulders a rough
cloak, secured at the waist. He stands on a ledge of rock at
the river's ford, and with impassioned voice and action, de-
nounces, exhorts, entreats, as now one, now another, now a
group, receive from him a mystic sign, then gather round him.

There is a hush. His eagle eye discerns among the crowd,
yet apart from it, a young man in peasant garb, who draws
nigh, and stands beside him. His long flowing hair is in color
"like the gold of Ophir." There is that in him that attracts
and binds one as by some magic force. Love and power seem
to flow out from the very face and form—a form of majesty,
yet of graciousness; a face, soft, appealing, full of love and
holy purpose, yet with all the power of command and will.
The loud, stern tones of the teacher's voice become low, sweet,
and tender, as he seems to plead with the stranger.

NOTE.—For one instant of that far-off history, Melchizedek stands before us, in the grandeur of his character and office, and in imme-diate relation to the Most High. After two thousand years he reap-pears in the Person of Christ, con-secrated a Priest, by the word of Jehovah. and the anointing of the Holy Spirit at his baptism.

REV. J. THOMPSON, D.D.

BIBLE SCENE, No. 2.

WE are in the farthest bounds of the Asian world, shut in from the nations around, by mountain ranges on the north and a dry desert of sand and rock on the south; the great sea on one side, deserts impassable but by caravan on the other. One long stretch of mountain country, intersected by winding, steep, narrow valleys, yet everywhere well-watered, and fruitful as the Garden of Eden. In this land, prepared by God, the story of a race begins, unrivalled in the world's history. It is four hundred and fifty years after the deluge, nineteen hundred before the coming of the Christ. We come by a mountain path, winding here and there, to a plateau that rolls up into hills, and still higher hills, swelling into mountain ridges that skirt the horizon, their snowy heads glistening in the sunlight. There is no highway of travel, no fence or enclosure. The virgin soil is rich in pasturage for the thousands of cattle and sheep that, gathered into droves, each in the care of herdsmen, are seeking shelter from the noonday heat in the shadows of the hillsides and the dark shade of olive groves native palms, and great oaks, scattered over the plain. Half hidden under these trees are hundreds of small black tents, and here, on the western side, overlooking the encampment, under a giant oak that casts shadow one hundred feet around, is a

large, double tent, open in front. Its richer appointments, the
tall, feathered spear before it, the beautiful Arab mares pick-
eted near, tell us that the grand old man seated there is the
master and owner of all this wealth. He is one hundred years
old to-day, but his long, flowing beard and whitened hair alone
tell of age. His childlike trust and repose in the God he worships has smoothed away all lines of care from his face. Living
as in the presence of his God, in constant communion and fel-
lowship, has brought back to him the image of God.

To-day, through the noonday glare and heat, he sees coming to him three men, unattended and on foot. The sheen of
their flowing white raiment is unsoiled by the dusty way.
They seem like a bright vision, half unreal. But they are not
so to the old man in the tent door. He hastens to meet them,
brings them into the cool shelter, provides for them a royal
feast, and as he stands to serve them he wakes as from sleep to
know that the One upon whom the two wait in silent reverence is no stranger. He is the *Presence* he has long loved and
worshipped, whose guidance he has followed all the years of
his exile. He has seen him in vision, he has entered into
special covenant with him, a covenant and promise sealed by
solemn sacrifice. From yonder hill he can see the valley
where, returning from victorious war, he first met him face to
face, as Priest and King, and received from his hands the bread
and wine, the symbol and shadow of his atoning sacrifice two
thousand years after.

And now again is the promise and covenant renewed. He stands with his Lord, looking down into that lovely valley embosomed in verdure, the rich fruitage creeping up the hills on either side of the river, and pleads with him as friend with friend, and is granted all he asks.

Dawn is breaking over the mountains. The old chieftain rises early and seeks the place where yesterday he stood. The valley lies there in its beauty and stillness, its waters sparkling in the morning light. On the plain beyond, behold! the two silent, white-robed visitants of yesterday hastening the reluctant flight of four figures he but dimly sees. Even as he looks a black cloud gathers over the plain; flames burst from beneath, and rising to heaven, fall back in sulphurous rain, and "the smoke of all that fair country goes up like the smoke of a furnace."

BIBLE SCENE, No. 3.

MORNING at last! The stars have gone out of the sky, the sun has flashed radiant to the zenith, and sends down its first fiery rays out of the cloudless white   It lights up with sudden splendor the marble palaces of a royal city, and the lowly roofs of its toil-worn and suffering serfs.   It falls on the dark waters of the river, and they sparkle in rose and silver sheen.

There, amid the rank growth on its banks, a lovely infant slumbers, and close beside, hidden by sheltering trees, a little girl stands watching.   Not yet has the morning light chased away the terrors of the darkness, for the night has been damp and chill, and to her quickened sense, all horrid things have come up out of the waters at her feet.   Since midnight she has stood there, fearsome and alone.

Many years are past.   The sun has set upon a countless multitude, encamped by the shore of a great sea.   It is mid-night; there are sounds on the air, sounds as of a mighty army, rushing horses, and mounted men, and clanging armor, and before it a flying host on foot, unarmed, undisciplined,

(10)

slavish with fear. And now with the morning light a voice is heard over the sea, and that proud army in all its brave array has gone down before its breath. The voice of the waters mingles with the song of the rescued host, led by the prophetess of God, and by the chosen leader and commander of his people—the little girl and the babe by the river-side.

BIBLE SCENE, No. 4.

PART I.

A WIDE plain, rich in all the vegetation of the tropics. The green flush of spring in the deep shadows, and crimson tints on the near mountains that surround this garden of the East.

Rising like an amphitheatre from the plain—a city of palaces; its busy, crowded streets, shaded on both sides with tall, graceful palm-trees. In the gardens the low, many-branched pomegranates, with their bell-shaped, reddish blossoms intermingled with the fragrant balsam and rich, flowering oleander, spikenard, and myrrh and camphire, with all sweet spices, fill the air with sweet odors.

It is a walled city, with watch-towers and buttresses, and watered by three great streams from the mountains. Farther out, near the suburbs, are groves of fig and olive trees; the houses are more scattered, and one so close against the city wall, you can step from its upper window upon it. Just here, outside the wall, are deep ravines, choked with jungle and canebrake, leading up to the mountains.

It is a lovely day in April. Two men in foreign dress leave this house, or inn, and walk through the city, noting the size

(12)

and strength of its walls, lingering beside street groups of excited talkers, until suspicious looks are turned to them, and they hasten back to the inn. They hold hurried counsel with its mistress, then she leads them to a hiding-place.

There is a loud knocking at the door; a mob of excited citizens have traced the strangers to the inn. Quietly the woman turns their search another way. She has left the girdle of her loose dress with the two men, and securing it to the casement they escape over the wall, through the tangled pass, to the mountains.

PART II.

A SWIFT-FLOWING river, famous in the history of an ancient people, owners, by gift, of all the land, on both sides, from the mountains to the sea. They are encamped—a great host—on its eastern bank. On the other side rises the proud city; sentinels are doubled on its walls; eager, terrified groups crowd the streets, the house-tops, the towers.

The camp is in motion. Six hundred thousand men march down to the river, swollen now by the spring rains, and rolling in dark, troubled surges far over the plain.

Look! an invisible hand has heaped the waters to one side, and down into the bed of the river, and up the western bank the whole army pass and encamp before the doomed city.

Days go by in imposing religious rites, and again the tread of the mighty host is heard. Forty thousand stately warriors lead them on. Priests, in richly embroidered robes, each with a silver trumpet, go before a mystic symbol, held aloft with its purple pall. Sixty thousand armed men close behind it. The trumpets sound, and the great army moves on ; no sound is heard, save their heavy tread and those trumpet tones.

Successive days the besieged look out upon this vast, silent procession. The Sabbath dawns, the whole host join in the solemn march. There is a sudden hush and halt, then a long trumpet blast. With arms thrown aloft, the leader gives the signal cry, and, like the roar of many waters, bursts forth from myriad voices the glad, exultant shout.

The earth trembles, heaves, the massive walls lie prostrate. Out, through the dead and dying, a woman and her friends are led to the victors' camp.

BIBLE SCENE, No. 5.

THE youngest in a family of ten, his name (in its significance The Beloved) is borne by no other in sacred history; tenderly loved by his father and only sister, he is tyrannized over and disliked by his brothers—bold, handsome, reckless men.

The boy is beautiful, slight and sinewy, his feet like the hinds upon the high places of the hills. Living for many days and nights in the open air, he sees in calm and storm and starry sky, the Divine power and presence, and his wondrous gift of song has strengthened, soothed, and cheered as none other in all time.

He leads a varied life. Now roaming the wild uplands with his flocks; now (yet a boy) in attendance upon the king; again, a child in his father's house; yet again honored at court; the idol of the people, their anointed Leader; now hunted through the land, an outlaw for years, yet keeping his child heart through all.

It is a wild scene we look upon; a dark, cavernous gorge, hid in the face of a cliff; a beetling wall of rock rising high above; a wild descent of rock and ruin deep below. The air within is close and oppressive; four hundred grim warriors are gathered round their young chieftain, tossing restlessly upon the rude bed they have made for him ; fever burns in every vein, his lips are parched with dust and thirst, visions of his boyhood's home—but a few miles away—come to him.   He longs for the cool, bright water from the well by the gate.

Out of the cave, and down the steep and stony track, three mighty men run swiftly, cutting their way through an armed garrison as they near the well.   And now, by aid of sling and helmet, they bear back the precious draught.   But to that royal heart it has become sacred as the blood of sacrifice.

BIBLE SCENE, No. 6.

WE go back in time—two thousand five hundred years—and stand upon the battlements of a city famous in Eastern story. Her walls, inclosing a vast plain, are sixty miles in circuit, of immesne height and thickness, surmounted by two hundred and fifty towers, a city of one hundred brazen gates, finely wrought in pictured history. Through the centre of the city a great river flows, spanned by a bridge of solid masonry, at each extremity of which rises a palace, seeming with their gardens to cover miles of ground. A city symbolical in the Apocalypse for wickedness, cruelty, pride, luxury, and idolatry. By river and by caravan she controls the commerce of all the Eastern world, and by conquest and traffic has gathered to herself the wealth of all lands.

In the great plain, on this day, are gathered Officers of State the world over. From lands most remote they have come, of every shade of complexion, in all styles of richest attire, to pay homage to the ruler, who holds in his one person a world-wide monarchy.

His statue, covered with plates of gold, from which the sun's rays are reflected back with dazzling splendor, rises ninety feet above the heads of the multitude summoned to attend the solemnity of its dedication.

On one side, but in sight of the monarch seated on a throne, elevated above the crowd, we see a court or square, cut in the natural rock, making a wall on three sides, open in front. In the centre is the place of fire, the oven, in which the great statue was moulded. Around the vast arena the orchestra are massed, with all manner of instruments known in all lands.

A trumpet blast, and the mighty host standing in solid column as they rank, are hushed to silence. A herald proclaims, as the test of allegiance, the worship of the statue, deified in the person of the monarch. To refuse is treason.

And now the shock and crash of sounds, like an in-rolling sea, lifts and bows prostrate toward the idol, the whole vast assembly. Three men alone stand erect. Their nearness to the throne, the richness of their robes of brilliant and various colors, the embroidered girdle and turban, the chain and signet ring, are badges of high office in the service of the monarch; their noble bearing and rare beauty is that of a foreign but royal race.

The king commands, and the men are brought before him. The ordeal is repeated, and the answer comes; they will worship no god, but the God of their fathers. What stays the king's wrath? Once more the test shall be tried; they may recant. Unmoved, untroubled, they meet it. To them there is but one God. The world is looking on, " Will their God deliver them? " See them bound, all unresisting as they stand, and thrust into the centre of the heat, fanned to fiercer flame.

What sees the monarch? " The angel of the Lord comes

down and smites the flame of the fire out of the oven and makes the midst of it as it were a moist whistling wind," and the four walk unharmed within the wall of fire. In the solemn awe and hush, the king again commands, and the three stand before him.

And now the decree goes forth. And the great multitude of every language take back over all the earth the first faint knowledge of the one living God—*God the Saviour*.

BIBLE SCENE, No. 7.

PART I.

TWO men—wholly unlike each other—chosen and set apart by God to do his work in times of great wickedness and great suffering.

One—a lonely man, living apart from men—in the solitudes of the desert, or the caves of the mountains, faring, no one knew how; his long shaggy hair, and a cloak of skins his clothing; feared by all, hated as well as feared by the wicked king and his heathen wife—hunted as an outlaw, but never found; yet when unsought, appearing to rebuke and warn, and departing unharmed; never but once asking a favor, and then, of a poor woman of another country; challenging to contest four hundred revilers of his faith, and gaining a signal victory. His going out of the world was unlike that of other men, and his name for years is linked with every event in church and state. Eight years after, a letter written by him is brought to the reigning king, foretelling his fearful death. Nine hundred years after, the typical prophecy of his return is fulfilled.

PART II.

THIS stern, strong man standing almost alone amid the profligacy of the times, has one devoted follower and friend,

who inherits his sole earthly possession, his spirit and his mission. He is a gentle, kindly man, in dress and manners like
other men, living like them in a home of his own. The coun-
sellor of the king and chief men of the nation, yet often sharing
with the poorest their rude lodging and hard fare. Giving up
all his worldly estate for the service of God, he yet attains to
great honor and distinction, using his influence to heal, and to
bless. Directing the schools of his order, he inspires them with
his own zeal. Living in close communion with God, he saves,
by the power given him, three armies from perishing of thirst,
and feeds one hundred men with a few loaves of barley bread.
One instance of severity in the beginning of his work, kept
unmolested his long after-life. One strange event, a year from
its close, is chronicled six hundred years after, in the legends
of his people, thus:

> " No word could overcome him,
> And after his death, his body prophesied:
> He did wonders in his life,
> And at his death, were his works marvellous."

BIBLE SCENE, No. 8.

H E is a Prince, of royal line, born in exile, brought up at court in the land of his captivity, promoted to personal service for the king; yet learned in the lore of his own people, and devoted to the faith and traditions of his fathers. In a heathen country, the centre of the world power, he remains a devout worshipper of the one true God.

The royal banquet is over for the time, the revellers are gathered in the garden court, or reclining on ivory couches, inlaid with gold and silver, in the grand colonnade, open to the sky. The floor is of variegated marble, curtains of finest damask and brilliant colors hang from the polished pillars.

The king and his beautiful queen are within the palace. The young Prince enters with a jewelled cup that he washes in their presence. Pouring some wine into his left hand, he drinks it, and filling the cup, presents it with courtly grace to the king.

The dark eyes of the young man tell of a sadness he does not seek to hide. Suspicious of harm, the king questions him. Emboldened by the presence and sympathy of the queen—like himself an exile—and by swift heart-appeal to the God he worships, he prefers his request.

It is the pleasant spring-time; provided with letters of

credit and an armed escort, our young Prince has made the long, perilous journey to the land of his fathers, once powerful and renowned, now an obscure province of the great empire he serves.

Midnight; a single horseman with a few attendants, passes silently through the dark, narrow streets of the city, out and in through its broken-down gates, taking a secret survey of its ruined walls and towers, until forced to return, by the piles of loose stones that give no foothold to his beast.

With the morning dawn, the elders of the city are assembled; credentials are shown, large contributions are freely made, women leading in the gifts. Detachments of men, each under its leader, begin the work of rebuilding, by solemn religious ceremonies.

And now come dissensions and evil rumors from without. Half the builders are withdrawn for sentry duty; even then workmen are armed. Our young ruler is among them, ever watchful day and night, a trumpeter beside him to give warning of alarm. Refusing the princely income from his government while absent from its duties, he yet supplies from his own resources the daily wants of one hundred and fifty of his most destitute subjects.

By his undaunted courage and vigilance, he defeats the plots of open violence or stratagem of his enemies. Inspiring his workmen with his own religious zeal, the walls are raised upon their old foundations in fifty-two days.

And now the sacred city—the city of the Great King—is dedicated anew to him, as its rightful Ruler. In solemn ceremonial the leading authorities, with a great orchestra, summoned from all parts of the country, and a vast concourse of people, march in imposing procession around the walls, pausing at intervals to engage in united prayer and praise.

At the central gate, the princes of the people, the priests and musicians are divided into two companies, and ascending the walls, walk, one to the right, the other to the left, with responsive chant, and the music of silver trumpets, meeting at the house of God, which they enter with solemn service and great rejoicing.

And so for twelve years our Prince is active reforming abuses, fortifying the city, sanctifying holy things, making provision for the religious instruction of the people, and the permanent support of religious service. Recalled for the second time to his place at court, he returns again, to give his latest years to work for God and his country.

In the legends of his people it is recorded that he sought and found the sacred fire hidden at the first destruction of the city and restored it to the altar in the holy place ; and that he collected and endowed a library, to which he added his own memoirs, that remained until the final overthrow of the city, more than five hundred years after.

And so endeth the story of the last historian of Bible times, before the advent of the Christ.

BIBLE SCENE, No. 9.

Part I.

A VAST plain, rich in historic memories, the battlefield of almost every nation under heaven.

Standing here, amid the ruins of a once royal city, we see the open space by its gates where its haughty, wicked queen met her dreadful death, and trace the scene of many a battle over the whole plain.

On that level ground, to the south, are grouped (more than three thousand years ago) nine hundred war-chariots and horses, with the princes of an invading army; on that higher ground are the vast host of their armed men. Before their camp flows the peaceful river, noted for all time in the war-songs of an ancient people, the rightful owners of the land. On that hill are mustered ten thousand of their mighty men under a female commander. They meet in battle; and now a storm bursts from the east, blinding the invading foe. The mountain torrent swells the river, turns their camping-ground into a swamp, and throws the countless host into wild and inextricable confusion.

(25)

Fifty years pass. Hordes from the desert come up, numerous as the sands of the sea. The peaceful dwellers of the plain flee to the caves of yonder mountain for safety. At its base, beside its mountain stream, their leader tests his men.

It is midnight; and the little band of three hundred, unarmed, march silently down to the enemy's camp. The signal is given; trumpet-sound and rallying-cry startle the sleeping warriors. They see bewildering, glittering lights, and hear the shouts of victory from unseen foes. Panic-stricken, each man mistakes his neighbor for his foe, and in wild terror they rush headlong down the valley.

Two hundred years—and again hostile hosts are marshalled on the plain. The first king of that ancient race, forsaken of God, conscience-stricken, returns from his midnight tryst, weary and heavy-hearted. Seven hundred thousand men meet at daybreak in the shock of battle. On the heights yonder, that noble form is stricken down, and beside him, true to the death, his more royal son.

Four hundred years—and the great battle is fought, typified in the Apocalyptic vision. The glory of that ancient people fades with the fall of their last great king, held in honor yet by yearly memorial rites.

In our own day, within the century, that *first* great battle is repeated. A vast army is put to utter rout by a few troops on their march over that great highway.

PART II.

IT is a sultry day in early harvest-time ; we stand on the slope of this hill, overlooking the great highway, where armies have pitched their tents for four thousand years.

Troops of reapers are gathering to the cornfields, scattered over the plain. Women follow to glean and bind the sheaves ; their bright Eastern dress, softened in the morning light, their shrill voices mingling with the song of birds as they meet and greet each other. At the head of the reapers the master walks, leading by the hand his only child. The hours pass, and the boy plays among the sheaves, but the sun rises higher and its fiery rays fall upon the boy's uncovered head.

A cool, dark room, the shaded light from a partly drawn screen reveals a ceiling broken by great rafters. A tiled floor, a few stools with carved legs, a low divan partially covered with a fringed quilt or shawl. There sits the mother, alone with her dead.

But now a great hope awakens in her heart.

With calm, set face she carries the little burden to a small room apart on the roof, lays him on the narrow bed, straightens the shapely limbs, folds the waxen hands, stands for a moment at the small lattice, looking far away across the plain to the mountain by the sea.

She is mounted now, driving fast and hard. Every living thing has sought shelter at this high hour of noon. The pit-

iless sun pulses with fierce heat over the shadeless plain. Un-
heeding she presses on, nor once draws rein. Somewhere in
that mountain covert is the help she seeks.

Again—over the hot, dusty plain, the long miles stretching
on and on, she returns, but not alone.

And now it is the cool eventide. The boy, in the full flush
of health, is hushed into happy quiet by the solemn awe and
gladness that fills the house.

Millions of men slain on that battlefield are forgotten as
they passed away. The soul of one little child given back from
the land of shadows and silence finds record on the sacred page,
which is told in story and in song all down the ages.

"And I say unto you, The hour is coming, when the dead
shall hear the voice of the Son of God, and they that hear shall
live. For the hour is coming, in the which all that are in the
graves shall hear his voice, and shall come forth, they that have
done good, unto the resurrection of life, and they that have
done evil, unto the resurrection of condemnation."

BIBLE SCENE, No. 10.

A LITTLE village, nestled high up among hills that are terraced in broad steps descending to the valley below, and clothed with fig-trees, olives, pomegranates, and vines. From their summits can be seen in the near distance the breastworks and battlements of strong fortresses, and the clear waters of a great sea.

It is early morning. From one of its flat-roofed, white-walled houses a young woman appears, an infant child in her arms. Beside her is a man much older. Carefully held in his hands is the symbol of a sacred offering.

The dress of both is a long, loose mantle or cloak, confined at the waist by a belt over a tight-fitting undergarment. The woman's is of finer texture, blue in color, and reaches to her sandalled feet. She is young and beautiful; her auburn tresses flow unconfined; the long, thick veil but partially covers her face and breast. It is gathered up and wrapped about the child.

Passing down the steep, narrow street, they go out at the town-gate, stop at an ancient well, shake the dust from their loose garments, and drink of its cool, delicious water.

They are now in a broad, deep valley, along whose rocky channel a stream flows. Now they pass a royal garden where two valleys meet. Mansions, gardens, and palaces rise on the hills beyond, and over there in dazzling splendor the royal porch of a grand temple, built upon solid masonry sheer up from the valley below. They are now in the narrow streets of a great city, and thread their way to a long flight of steps leading up to a great gate glistening in the morning light.

Passing through a court in which hang thousands of bucklers and shields of mighty men slain in battle, they come to another gate, high and massive, richly carved, and glowing as if on fire. Through this, and crossing the bright inlaid pavement, they ascend low, crescent-shaped steps to a higher court and wait. Before them is an inner building of pure white marble; about it many men in priestly garb.

And now has come to pass the legend told four hundred years before, and though unseen, the glory of the Triune Presence fills the place.

BIBLE SCENE, No. 11.

A PATHWAY, six miles in extent; old as the hills over which it winds; steep and narrow in its descent; wild and devious under the shadow of rocky cliffs, or broadening over the plain. Now but a footpath among the oaks and across the green cornfields, where three thousand years ago the mother of a royal Line, followed the gleaners. At intervals, we catch glimpses of a wild landscape,—rugged hills and deep glens, and, skirting the horizon, a ruddy line—the crest of a walled city.

Along this road, four thousand years ago, a grand old man and his son, in the loose rich dress of the nobles of those times, are nearing the end of their journey. As it comes in sight they dismount, and father and son go on alone and on foot, to the place—now, and for centuries past, and for all time, the most sacred and endeared on earth.

A hundred years and more go by, and we travel this same road again, with an old man, returning with his family and servants to his father's home. The man is lame, and rides beside a litter, upon which is borne a dying woman. He hopes to reach the little city, now but a mile away, but here the ascent is sharp and steep; and in that narrow valley the woman dies and is buried.

(31)

Seven hundred years are told, and once more we visit this pathway, to find it filled with armed men, seeking a hiding-place in the fortresses of its rocks. Mighty men, in mailed armor, are in attendance upon their chief, and as the days wear on, the aged and the young—men of all ranks—from all the country round, gather about him. Scarce fifty years are past, and of all that brave army, a few old men are left ; but the land, in peace through all its borders, is famed through all lands, for its power and wealth and glory, and this tortuous path has become a royal carriage-way.

The years roll on—one thousand years—the glory of the nation has passed away. Of all that royal house, a few obscure families alone remain. Of these, a young woman, and a man much older, enter late one afternoon, this same pathway—the last stage of their toilsome journey. A few weeks later, and they again tread the path, bearing an infant child. Again a few years, and that infant of days, now a man, forsaken, insulted, bowed with suffering—the victim of mob riot, civil riot, priest riot—is offered up to death.

BIBLE SCENE, No. 12.—THE HISTORY OF AN OLD HOUSE IN BIBLE TIMES.

IT is a large, stone house, built on stone arches, through which the cattle are led to their stalls, or grottoes in the hillside, against which it stands, and at the head of a long, narrow, steep street that runs up from the ravine below the town. Save a low doorway and a small latticed window, it presents a dead wall to the street.

We enter this doorway and find ourselves in a small audience-room ; with little furnishing beside the low divan around it. A private stairway leads from this room to a wide gallery, that extends around and looks down into a large square court, part garden, part a pavement of variegated marble. We find the house is built around this court ; all its rooms open upon the gallery. A second stairway leads to the flat roof and parapet overhanging, and supported by columns.

The rooms are spacious, some of them richly furnished. From the carved ceilings hang curtains of brilliant colors and finest texture, drawn or put aside at will. The floors, of pictured tiles, are covered with rich rugs, as are the low couches or divans around the walls.

To this house, thirty-five hundred years ago, a prince of the tribe of Judah brought his foreign bride. She had saved his life, embraced his faith, and forgot in the quiet of her new life, and the training of her boy, the sorrows of the past. The boy, grown to manhood, takes his father's place and rank.

It is early harvest-time ; two women have come to the little village, and the whole place is astir. Old memories are recalled of the one, now feeble and aged, returned to the home of her youth, but the fair hair and blue eyes of the younger woman tell of her foreign birth. They have come from beyond the dark sea, across the rich plains by the storied river, through mountain glens and lonely desert paths, to find a home here. They are poor and friendless, and the younger stranger toils through the long hot days, in the fields of the grave, good man, now master at the great house. The days go by and she becomes his wife.

Two hundred and fifty years pass. One day an old man, in the garb of a priest, toils up the steep stony street to this house on the hill-top. The great-grandson of that young stranger, himself an old man, greets him with reverent homage. Seven stalwart sons are about him ; his youngest, "the darling," is away on the hills. He enters at his father's call, and the old priest lays his hands in consecration upon the head of the beautiful boy.

The years wear on with their many changes. The boy, now a worn-out, aged man, is laid at rest with his fathers, and the whole land mourns for the grandest king that ever filled a throne.

Four hundred and fifty years are gone. The land is desolate, her cities and temples in ruin, her king and nobles in captivity. In the strong old house, a prophet of their God finds refuge.

Again five hundred years. Cities and temples are rebuilt, but the land is under foreign rule. The descendants of its kingly race are scattered and impoverished. The old stone house, in its decay, has become the village inn.

The short winter day is closing in, as two weary travellers toil up the steep broken street to their ancestral home. They find no room. The night air is cold, and groping their way through the cloistered arches, they seek warmth and shelter in the hillside grotto.

It is midnight; the moon has risen, but a glory far above its radiance fills the place. All heaven is gazing down, for to our sin-burdened earth its Saviour has come, " Emmanuel, God with us."

BIBLE SCENE, No. 13.

IT is the bright spring month of the year, the song of birds
floods all the air, the valleys and plains are covered with
rich green, and the gray hills are lit up with a hundred glories,
for it is the month of flowers.

And it is the season of a great national festival. Multitudes
have come up to the capital from every part of the land, and
from lands remote. Three millions of people crowding, strug-
gling through its narrow streets, filling the houses, camping on
the house-tops and in the courts. Outside the walls the valleys
and hillsides are black with tents.

The one point of attraction, where for a thousand years the
daily worship has been offered, stands out in dazzling splendor
against the sky a wilderness of columns, and arches, and courts.
Built upon a bold, sharp promontory, walled up from the valleys
on either side, sheeted with gold, it shines resplendent from all
parts of the city.

On this day, the 14th of April, the outer enclosure of the
sacred edifice is changed into a cattle fair, the loud traffic mingling with the prayer and chant of the inner courts. Amid this
Babel of tongues, and thronging, jostling crowd of men and
beasts, the buying and selling, and money-changing going on, a
stranger enters—a young man in the simple garb of a peasant,

(36)

but with something majestic in his face and bearing. He looks around with indignant sorrow. Strands of hempen cord are scattered on the marble floor. With a few gathered up, he protests, in his Father's name, against the desecration of his Father's house.

The power and authority of eye, and voice, and action is a spell upon the crowd. At the touch of that slender scourge the court is cleared. No resistance is offered ; a sudden, mysterious, irresistible awe is upon them all.

The excitement draws from the inner court the officers and priesthood. Here is one who claims an authority above their own.

In this group of lookers-on is a man of advanced age, high in rank and office in college, church, and state. As he watches the stranger, memories are stirred of another such sacred festival eighteen years before, when, seated in his hall of learning, his friends in office around him, a strangely attractive, thoughtful boy had entered, and seated at his feet, had asked and answered questions with such wisdom and grace that his heart was drawn in loving-kindness to him, and held him in close companionship two days and nights.

Among the art treasures his great wealth had gathered, were relics and legends of their most worshipped king, and *this* boy was of that royal line ; his record was clear. His sacred books told of One in direct descent, who should restore the ancient glory of his people, and reign a Prince and Saviour over all the world. How often he had pored over these records with long-

ing desire for the coming of the Deliverer. In the stranger before him, so gracious yet so commanding, he sees the *boy* never
forgotten. He had heard of wondrous signs attending the
stranger's appearing, of wondrous *acts*, as of one clothed with a
divine commission, and now he speaks of a life, an eternal life,
a life he is longing to realize. He must know more; he must
see him apart from the crowd. But when? Where?

And now he observes a young man attendant upon the
stranger, taking no part in his act, but following him with loving reverence. He knows the man well. His father, though
plying his trade at a distance, owns a house near the city wall;
the stranger may be found there. A few hurried words, a signal
of silence, and they are lost in the press.

The sun has set, the moon not yet risen; the great lights
from the temple throw their radiance over the house-tops and
the more distant hills, leaving in dim shadow the narrow streets,
where many a weary, homeless pilgrim has sought rest, sheltered
by the dead walls. Avoiding these, passing stealthily through
by-lanes and alleys, a man muffled in a long cloak arrives at a
house near one of the city gates. A faint signal at the low door,
and it opens to admit him.

From that young follower, the historian of later years, we
learn of words spoken by the stranger that night to the anxious,
doubting, but honest seeker after the truth; words that have
changed the life and destiny of millions, and gone forth with
might and healing to every nation under heaven.

BIBLE SCENE, No. 14.

STANDING on the shore of a small inland sea, six hundred feet below the ocean level, and looking along the rocky valley that forms its basin, there come to us echoes from the old Hebrew seers:

> "The Lord thundered from heaven,
> And the Most High uttered his voice,
> The mountains saw him and were afraid,
> The everlasting hills did bow,
> The tempest of waters passed by,
> The valleys were cleft as wax before the fire."

In a far past age some great convulsion of nature must have reft apart this long chain of mountains, that falling to the east and west, left this deep hollow, now a lovely lake, crystal-like in its clearness, fringed with flowering oleanders, and alive with boats. On either side vast plateaus, to a great height, spread backward and upward. Cities upon the hills—the hollows in the hillsides set with hamlets, vineyards, groves of figs, olives, and fruits of every clime. The landscape on this side is full of life; towns, cities, and villages crowd the shore, full of a restless, busy people; terraced hills, covered with trees, higher hills rising beyond. Across the lake a long strip of pasture-land, beyond which rise distant hills, gray, barren, and desolate.

Just here, at the head of the lake, in a region of unequalled beauty, lies a little city, the halting-place of travellers from the farthest boundaries of Cæsar's empire. The great Roman road bends here, over which pass the caravans to Italy, India, Scythia, and Ethiopia, opening the markets of the world to the products of the vineyards, orchards, and fisheries of the lake.

To this busy little city a stranger has come, whose mysterious claims and wondrous acts of power and of healing are rumored all over the land. His home is with two of his followers, in one of those small, whitewashed houses by the sea. The low door opens into a large, low room, with no furnishing save a few stools that serve as tables, and a bench or divan around three sides, covered with rugs, the common resting-place, by day and night, of all in the house.

Yesterday the crowds around it and filling the narrow streets all the long day, pressed heavily upon the stranger, whose simple word, or the touch of whose hand brought healing to the sick and life even to the dead. Evening came at last, but the rest he needed could not be gained in the stifling air of that crowded room, and long before day he sought the solitude of the seaside for strength and prayer.

The dawning light this morning revealed him walking upon the narrow beach ; a man of middle size, in the dress of his time and country. A square of white linen covers the long hair that falls in wavy luxuriance to his shoulders. A seamless tunic reaches to his sandalled feet ; over this a long, blue robe or cloak, with loose, flowing sleeves. His features are of the Grecian type, blended with the Jewish into a perfect beauty, that awakens reverence and love. His eyes, whose keen glance seem to read all hearts, are softened, as if looking through tears. There is about him a native dignity and grace, like one who knows himself a King. A man, apart from men, yet as one taking the whole world to his heart.

The fishermen are coming in from their night's toil on the lake, and the busy multitude are astir in the town. They shout to each other and are answered back in loud, harsh tones, which, mingled with the sharp, high voices of the women as they meet and greet each other, make a very Babel of tongues. But now they descry the stranger, all else is forgotten. They gather closer and closer about him, until pressed to the water's edge, he steps into a boat, and resting on the swaying seat, patiently and kindly talks to the rude or curious, or earnest multitude on the land. It is a motley crowd. Peasants and priest; Greek merchant and Roman soldier; the blind, and lame, and sick of yesterday, now in the full vigor of health. From the common forms of life around him he gathers truths that will live and grow with quickening power, changing customs, thought, and life, until the will of God, as done in heaven, becomes the pattern of life on earth.

The heat of noon scatters the crowd, and the stranger returns to the house, where the simple noonday meal is spread— thin cakes of barley bread, a few olives, or figs, perchance fish from the lake, cooked in oil—but his followers gather about him with other earnest seekers after truth, and give him no leisure to eat. Through the sultry afternoon he continues to teach them, and evening finds him once more at the seaside. In the gathering darkness, overpowered by the need of rest and sleep, without food or added raiment, he seeks the quiet and solitude of the eastern shore. At last he can lay his weary head upon the steersman's seat and sleep the deep sleep of exhaustion.

It has been a warm, bright day in early spring, but the night grows chill. They are in the midst of the sea, and a sudden tempest sweeps down with fierce fury upon the lake. The icy wind and sleet beat about the rowers with such force, no effort of theirs can bring the boat to shore at any point. The foam of the breakers dashes over her and covers the stranger with the spray; yet he sleeps on, undisturbed by the darkness and tempest. They are strong men, accustomed to the oar, but the wild wind howls down through the mountain gorges with resistless fury, and sweeps them far away from their course. Their strength is exhausted, the danger becomes extreme. Wild voices mingle with the shrieks of the winds and the dash of the waves and fill them with terror. Their cries awake the sleeper. He rises in his calm majesty, gazes out into the darkness, and his voice, above the raging of the tempest, with the Almightiness of conscious power, rebukes the Evil Spirit in the winds and stills the waves to rest. The stars shine brightly down from the clear sky, the awed boatmen bend in silence to the oar, and the little vessel glides swiftly over the placid waters.

Who is this man, but now so worn and weary, so human in his needs, who, standing on the sinking ship in the darkness of night and tempest, by one word rules to silence the raging fiend in the storm and hushes the sea to rest? Again echo from the Hebrew prophet answers:

> " Unto us a child is born,
> Unto us a Son is given, and
> His name shall be called Wonderful,
> The Mighty God, the Prince of Peace."

BIBLE SCENE, No. 15.

THE air is sharp and chilly this winter morning, as three men start at daybreak for a rapid walk of six miles, to reach their trysting-place at noon. The rough stones over which lay their path are slippery with frost, but as the sun rises higher, the slime from melting ice, and clay soil, taxes all their strength to keep a sure footing along the tortuous path that leads them over hills, and steep descents, through narrow passes, and freshly ploughed fields.

The last hour's walk is over. A wide plain, broken by the plough, lies bare and shadeless in the sun. Just where the mountain range is cleft from summit to base, and at the entrance of the vale between, is an ancient well, by which they stop to rest.

One of the travellers can go no further. The toil of days and nights in his chosen mission has not dimmed the matchless beauty of face and form, or ruffled the heavenly calm of his spirit, but he is faint and weary, and he knows that here will be gathered his first harvest from an alien race.

His companions are of coarser mould, hardened to greater endurance. Leaving him beside the well, they walk on to the city yet a mile away. His eyes follow the path they take up

(44)

the valley. A few weeks, and the terraced hillsides that now present but bare walls, and shelves of brown earth, will be robed in glorious beauty of waving green, and " precious fruits brought forth by the sun." He sees the place beneath the oaks where nearly two thousand years before the great father of their people erected the first altar to Jehovah in that land, and where he, that weary stranger at the well, met and blessed him.

On that same camping-ground, the old chieftain's grandson dwelt with his family, and servants, and flocks, and sunk the well that yet bears his name. And here, in after years, the son of *his* old age paused to drink of its cooling water; then with boyish haste went on his father's errand up that path through the parted hills, never to return in life. Yet, for more than three thousand years his coffined dust has lain buried here.

Midway up the valley, the stranger had seen the symbol of his covenant with this people, the centre of a great host of conquering tribes. On this side and on that, three hundred thousand voices, answering to as many more, while along the heights rolled the responsive Amen. And here their Leader, in the last act of his life, gathered the Princes of his people and erected in solemn covenant a witness of their allegiance to the one true God.

And now this silent noon, when no one else is abroad, a woman comes along to draw water from the sacred well. The stranger resting there knows it has no hidden charm to ease her troubled conscience, and he would take the weary weight and set her free.

And still from his lips, over all the world, the words are sounding forth—" If any man thirst, let him come unto me and drink "—and still those other voices are heard catching up and re-echoing the call--" Whosoever will, let him come and take of the water of life freely."

BIBLE SCENE, No. 16.

IT is afternoon at the close of an eventful week. In and
around the crowded city the millions have been stirred to
wild excitement. To-day strange rumors are abroad; people
hurry past with scared faces, or gather in little groups about
the streets. They do not notice one or two men who, as they
wind their way through the crowd, signal by word or look
many they meet, and that these, quietly, somewhat stealthily,
pass on and enter a house near the city gates. It is late this
afternoon, and two men of the company there convened take
leave of their friends, and are returning to their country home.
The trees are in full leaf, the hawthorn is laden with blossom
and fragrance along the Roman highway, for it is the sweet
spring-time. In the valley they now enter, flowers of every
hue fringe the cliffs of white limestone; crimson anemones and
white daisies are a carpet under their feet. But they pass un-
heeding; they do not see a stranger who has joined them. He
speaks, and as they walk he talks long and earnestly. They
half resented the stranger's greeting, but now they listen in
silence, pressing nearer to him, with eyes aglow and thoughts
too big for utterance. The village home is reached, the three
enter.

Scarce an hour is past; the two men are hurrying back over the same road, quiet and deserted now. They seem like men distraught; now in silent musing, now making the hills echo with their glad song. As they near the city they break into a run, and gain an entrance before the closing of the gates.

BIBLE SCENE, No. 17.

SEVEN men, bound to each other by the strongest ties of loving companionship and of loyalty to their Commander, have come at eventide to the shore of a great inland sea, where a small vessel and a boat are anchored. They have passed through strange scenes in a distant city, and now they are at home, awaiting their Master's promise to meet them there.

From the beautiful beach upon which they stand may be seen nine Roman and Greek cities. The sea itself, lying in a deep basin sixteen miles in extent, bears upon its bosom many ships of war and many of commerce, carrying fish of the choicest kinds, wine, wheat, fruits, and oil, the produce of its ports, to the markets of the south. A Roman road, five hundred miles in length, touches here by the sea, then bends to the south. Stretching along this road are caravans laden with merchandise for the oldest city in the world.

Numerous villages and hamlets dot the surrounding hillsides, that are terraced to their tops with trees and vines, save where the watercourses have cut deep ravines and wild gorges, through which the winds from the mountains sometimes rush, lashing the peaceful sea into sudden storm.

The men have entered the larger boat and pushed out from

the land, dragging the other at the stern, and night comes down upon the scene.

And now it is the gray dawn of morning, but as yet there is no light in the little hamlet earliest awake along the water-side, and the weary, hungry men see only the mist on the hill-tops as they pull their boat toward the nearest shore. There is a glow on the beach, and as they draw nearer a form is seen through the glimmering dusk. And now, over the water comes a voice clear and distinct in the still morning air. There is an instant change in the boat's crew, as with rapid movements and in reverent silence the order is obeyed.

BIBLE SCENE, No. 18.

IT stands, a tower-fortress, half palace, half castle, built of massive rock, with pillared courts, and baths and spacious barracks; the foundations of rock, seventy-five feet high, on each side a sheer precipice, overlaid with polished slabs of stone, giving no hold to foot or hand. Four other towers, of less or greater height, surround it. One—the dungeon keep— joins the colonnade of a great temple, about which an armed guard is always stationed. In and around the towers are battalions of Roman soldiers under arms.

In a cell of this high tower that is parted only by a deep rift in the precipitous rock from the temple courts, is a prisoner in chains. Sixteen armed soldiers, answerable with their lives for the safe keeping of this one man, hold watch within its guarded and bolted doors. To two of these the prisoner is chained. Day by day the thronged courts of the temple have rung with the grand symphony of thousands of silver trumpets and the choral harmony of chanting voices. And the music and the chant and the fragrance of incense have fallen on the sense of the lonely captive in the prison tower. But now the solemn rites of the last great day of the nation's sacred festival are ended. The city and the hills around, so lately vocal

with rejoicing millions, are silent. The watchmen have taken
their stand on the temple terrace, and on the castle-fortress
the Roman garrison have set their nightly guard. The cer-
tainty that in a few hours now he will suffer a painful death,
surrounded by a scoffing rabble, scarce stirs the sublime calm
of the captive, and he sleeps the healthful sleep of a strong
man, at peace with conscience and at rest in God.

In the ten years that have passed since he received the parting commission of his Master, he has faced death many times.
Each morning's watch, at the same hour of his great sin, he
has sought renewed forgiveness, and to-morrow he will see, face
to face, in glad and open vision, his glorified Lord.

A voice—the touch of a hand—awakes him. The cell is
ablaze with light. Half entranced he hears the command,
"Arise." He stands unbound. Again the voice; as in a dream
he obeys, yet sees only the glorious vision.

The iron doors are locked and guarded within and without,
but captive and guide have passed through them. They come
to the outer gate, it opens unseen, unheard by the armed
watchers, and they stand free of the castle. And now, down
the descent to the temple terrace. The soldiers, stationed at
every point, are passed as shadows, and they are in the silent
street; waking to consciousness, he is alone.

The moon has risen. The great lights from the temple
courts throw their splendor far out over the sleeping city
and the hills around, but so all unlike the brightness of that

vanished glory, he knows his angel visitant has set him free, and it is the Master's will that he take up the burden of life again. The years stretch out before him, years of toil, and pain, and exile. He sees himself a feeble old man, far from friends, led out to a shameful death; yet so will he be nearer and like his Lord. And now he must care for the life given back; that, too, is his Master's will. He will relieve the friends that are grieving and praying for him; but before the morning dawns he must be far away.

BIBLE SCENE, No. 19.

IT is a time of great persecution in the early church; many Christians have fled to distant cities.

A young man bearing dispatches, with soldiers under command, has journeyed for days over stony hills and desert plains, with here and there a glimpse of the sea; and now a snow-capped mountain, the landmark of his mission, comes in view. The weary men pause to drink from a well at the opening of a beautiful valley; again they are upon the barren uplands, under the burning sky, held on their course by their tireless leader. They gladly welcome the first glimpse of the ancient city they are nearing, in its green enclosure of beautiful gardens—a city older than the Patriarchs, famed in the chronicles of Israel's Kings, noted by her greatest prophet as Israel's "merchant in the multitude of its wares, in the multitude of all riches, in wine and wool." From oldest time to our day, it stands unchanged, the desert bulwark around it; the same "river of gold" keeping its garden in constant verdure.

Through these the white buildings now gleam in the noon-tide heat, for the hush of noon is over the city as the travellers draw near the gate.

What so alarms, stirs, bewilders them? An unseen hand arrests them. A glory from the opened heavens surrounds them. Their proud leader lies prostrate on the ground. He hears what they do not hear. He sees what they do not see. He rises subdued, remorseful, obedient. In utter darkness, trembling, helpless, he is led into the city.

BIBLE SCENE, No. 20.

.

A GRECIAN city famous in Roman history. Mingling with the crowds of Roman soldiers, citizens, and foreigners in its busy streets, are four men in the dress of an ancient but hated race. One, with the charm of youthful beauty and grace and culture. One, a much older man, with lines of thought and study in his thin face. One seemingly born to command, but close in attendance upon the leader of the party, a small, nervous man, with long, flowing, pointed beard, dark gray eyes shaded by contracted eyebrows, as if from defective sight; a high, bald forehead, a face betraying quick change of feeling, and marked with deep lines of suffering.

Outside the city little streamlets from the hillsides have met and mingled in a gently flowing river. On its banks is a small chapel, open to the sky. A few women have gathered there in the calm of a Sabbath morning for prayer. The four men enter, and to the eager listeners the leader tells the story of the Cross, and the first convert in Europe is gained for Christ.

BIBLE SCENE, No. 21.

A CITY of granite, all within its vast enclosure of colossal masonry built of the same gray stone. Here, a Greek temple commands a view of the sea. There, open arches of immense size tell of Roman builders.

In a large upper room of one of its homes, lighted by a projecting window or balcony overhanging the street, many people are gathered; a tender, sad, earnest look is on every countenance. It is evening before the Sabbath. A man of small, slight stature is addressing them; his face is of the Greek type, betraying quick changes of feeling, forehead high and bald, bright gray eyes under thickly fringed eyebrows, and a long, flowing beard.

On the morrow the vessel that is to bear him far away, it may be to death, will sail, and his friends are met to celebrate with him a parting feast of love and hear his farewell words. The night is dark, the moon but a faint crescent now, and many lamps are burning in the room.

There is a sudden stir, a cry, a heavy fall. In confusion and alarm, lights are flashing here and there; then, a few quiet words from the preacher, and all is calm again. Now they

(57)

gather round the board, spread for refreshment, and the Eucharistic Feast. The day dawns, they cannot part, a few hours may be gained and the vessel met at another point. At last he is left alone, hastening through the oak woods now in full leaf; now along the Roman road, he enters the street of tombs leading to the shore, where the vessel lies at anchor in the Roads.

BIBLE SCENE, No. 22.

A BAND of prisoners, walking along the most famous and frequented of all the roads known for more than two thousand years; each prisoner's right hand chained to that of a soldier on his left.

First in this band is a feeble old man, laboring to keep step with his guard, who seems kindly to favor him.

It is a warm spring day in that languid southern air, and the aged man has travelled thus for many days on foot. For weeks before he has been tossed upon a stormy sea; then cast upon a rocky coast.

Born to wealth and station among his own people, learned in their schools, a member of their highest court of judicature, in early manhood he had freely given up all for love of Christ, and lived a wanderer and a fugitive, laboring with his hands for support, spending the best years of his life in prison and exile; exposed to hunger, cold, and heat; often stoned and beaten by mob and priestly law, yet still, with the persistence of a great love, telling his mission of mercy in all the great centres of the known world, everywhere gaining converts to his faith. And now he comes, as he had long desired, to the world's capital, but as a prisoner in chains.

The great road is thronged with crowds of every clime and rank. No kindly word or glance is given the weary old man. All are strangers; even his friendly guard must soon leave him. He sees only a prison cell before him, and looks sad and downcast.

They are now in the narrow streets of a small town; through the motley crowd, the file of prisoners and soldiers slowly make their way. Suddenly, a cry of joy! A group of eager men, waiting, watching there, have come the long forty miles from the great city to meet and welcome the aged prisoner. How they gather round him, his own children in the faith, for whom he had labored in the distant cities of the East. With renewed hope he thanks God and takes courage.

The last rise of ground brings him in view of the city. A long line of blue mountains runs far out to the sea; villas and gardens cluster at their base; narrow roads lead to the vast mass of buildings twelve miles in circuit, with its millions of living souls. His heart is high, as he looks adown the years and sees churches planted, and heralds sent through all this region to tell the glad news of salvation through Jesus the Crucified, and the banners of the Empire blazoned with the image of the Cross.

Does he see, in nearer vision, this Gospel preached through him to all the Gentile world? Does he see his trial and release; his years yet of travel and exile; his return and martyrdom? The long struggle of truth and error; the "mystery of iniquity" holding rule alike in Pagan temple and Christian church? Does he see " the angel having the everlasting Gospel to preach to all that dwell on the earth," and hear the final acclaim, "The kingdoms of this world are become the kingdoms of our Lord and of His Christ "?

BIBLE SCENE, No. 23.

WE are in Rome, this twenty-ninth of June, in the year of our Lord sixty-six. The fires of persecution still burn hotly against the Christian church, and the gardens of Nero are still lighted by her martyrs.

Here, at the foot of the Capitoline Hill, near the Roman Forum, is a deep excavation in the rock, forming two chambers; the upper, far below the surface of the ground; the lower, entered only by a hole in the floor above; floor, roof, walls, all of stone, hollowed out of the solid rock six hundred years before.

Breathing the fetid air of this dungeon, that, seen by a taper's light, reveals slimy, noxious things, that fill one with horror, a prisoner has been for months confined, an old man of small and feeble frame, ever racked with pain. No change, no resting-place, no ray of sunlight, no breath of heaven's pure air; the cold, damp dungeon chills him to the heart; but an inner warmth and light is there, that turns the shadow of death into the morning.

To-day he is to be led out to a painful death, but the joy of that deliverance so soon to be his, fills heart and soul, as he sends his last message to his friends. A life ending in a dungeon, a death that of a malefactor, but the message is the Coronation hymn of a victor about to receive his crown.

At his trial, all forsook him; no advocate ventured to plead his cause; but then, as always, the Captain of the Lord's host stood by him. As seeing him who is invisible and strong in his strength, he had years before boldly proclaimed his faith in the courts of the Cæsars; he had unfolded the Gospel message to the crowd of philosophers on Mars Hill at Athens, and from the castle stairs at Fort Antonia preached to Jew and Gentile, Jesus and the resurrection. In his strength and for his sake, he had borne the scourge, the stocks, the violence of mobs, tedious journeys in cold and heat; shipwreck, hunger, imprisonment, was hated and hunted by his own brethren, and now again he stands, deserted by his friend, the iron forms of the Roman soldiers about him; judges, lictors, thousands of spectators, gazing upon one feeble old man, pleading his own cause.

Acquitted on the first charge, he is again remanded to prison, to await sentence for his avowed faith. The months of imprisonment yet before him, the tortures that might await him, the martyrdom he must surely suffer, have few terrors for him; but the human heart of the man longs for the friends now far away. One had sought and found him, and one—his loved physician, unmindful of fear or shame—is with him now. By his hand he has written his "dearly beloved child in the faith," urging him to come with all speed that he may see his

face once more. Is it too late? May he not be in this crowd
that follows the martyr and his executioners along the Ostian
road, threading their way through the dust and tumult of the
busy throng this midsummer day, out beyond the city walls?
In that crowd are many that love the grand old man. There
is one Bishop of a church in Rome; another, the son of a
Roman senator, with his bride, the daughter of a British king;
his faithful physician is there, and many another his children
in the faith; but the tortures they have witnessed have struck
terror into their otherwise true hearts. It matters not to the
old man now. Hurried on, chained to a soldier on either side,
he sees only his Lord, rejoicing to follow him even in death,
" without the gate."

The church in Heaven, to-day, welcomes the greatest victor
that ever won the race; the church on earth, to-day, had never
such cause to weep, since her Lord himself was led through
Calvary, to death.

KEY.

SCENE 1.—Christ as Melchizedek, meeting Abraham   Gen. xiv. 14-20.

Compare Ps. cx. 4; David, in saying that Christ was after the Order of Melchizedek, "a Priest forever," must mean in respect to its *eternity*, for upon the eternity of Christ's Priesthood the whole hope of the Christian rests.

Compare also Heb. v. 5, 6, and Heb. vii. 1-3, also 8th and 23d to 25th verses of the same chapter. Paul reasons that Christ could not have been a Priest after the Order of Aaron, because Aaron and the Priests succeeding him *died*. If Melchizedek died, how was he better than Aaron?

The meeting of Melchizedek with bread and wine, the emblems of Christ's human body, "broken for us," was at the very spot where, 2,000 years after, baptized of John in Jordan, He was anointed as our High-Priest, by the Holy Spirit descending upon Him. Matt. iii. 13-17; see also John viii. 56.

SCENE 2.—The second appearance of the Son of God as a Man to Abraham, and the destruction of the cities of the Plain. Gen. xviii. and Gen. xix. 15-17, 27, 28.

SCENE 3.—Moses and Miriam. Ex. ii. 1-4, xiv. 21-28, and xv. 20, 21.

SCENE 4.—David in the Cave of Adullam. 1 Chron. xi. 15-19.

SCENE 5.—Read Joshua, 2d chapter; iii. 14-17, and vi. 1-16, 25.

SCENE 6.—Elijah. 2 Kings i. 6-8, also 1 Kings xvii. 5, 6, 9-16, xviii. 19-38, and 2 Kings ii. 9-11.

Eight years *after* the translation of Elijah this writing was brought to Jehoram, King of Judah—2 Chron. xxi. 12-15, 19; nine hundred years after—Matt. iii. 1-3.

PART II.—ELISHA. 2 Kings ii. 12-15, 23, 24; also iii. 9, 17, 20, iv. 42-44, and xiii. 20, 21.

SCENE 7.—THE PLAIN OF ESDRAELON, IN OR NEAR WHICH WAS THE VALE OF MEGIDDO. Rev. xvi. 16.

Characters.—*Jezebel*, 2 Kings ix. 30-33; *Deborah*, Judges iv. 1-4, 13-15, and Judges v. 20-22; *Gideon*, Judges vi. 1-5, and Judges vii. 1-8, 16-22; *Saul*, 1 Samuel xxviii. 4-8, 15-20, and 1 Samuel xxxi. 1-6, also 2 Samuel i. 23-27; *Josiah*, 2 Chron. xxxv. 22-25; *Napoleon's* march to Egypt.

PART II.—Read 2 Kings iv. 8-37.

SCENE 8.—Read Daniel, 3d chapter.

SCENE 9.—ROYAL PALACE IN SHUSHAN, PERSIA.

Nehemiah, a Prince of the Tribe of Judah, born in captivity; *King Artaxerxes*, the same as Ahasuerus; *Esther* (a Jewess), his Queen. Read Nehemiah i. 1 and ii. 1-7, 9, 11-19; also iv. 16-20 and xii. 27-31, 38, 40.

SCENE 10.—THE PATHWAY BETWEEN JERUSALEM AND BETHLEHEM.

Abraham and *Isaac*, Gen. xxii. 1-6; *Jacob*, Gen. xxxv. 1, 16, 19; *David*, 1 Samuel xxii. 1, 2; *Solomon*, 1 Kings x. 26; *Joseph* and *Mary*, Luke ii. 3-7; *The Infant Christ, Mary* and *Joseph*, Luke ii. 22; *The Lord Christ*, bearing His cross to Calvary.

SCENE 11.—THE HOUSE OF CHIMHAM, supposed to be the Inheritance of King David. See 2 Samuel xix. 33, 37, 38, and 1 Kings ii. 7.

Salmon of the House of Judah and Rahab, see Matt. i. 4-6—compare Numbers x. 14; *Naomi* and *Ruth*, see Ruth i. 22 and iv. 13, 17; *Samuel*, see 1 Samuel xvi. 1, 4, 10-17; *David*, 1 Chron. xiv. 17 and 1 Kings

ii. 10 ; *Jeremiah* xxxix. 14 and xli. 17, 18 ; *The Infant Jesus*, Luke ii. 7–11.

SCENE 12 (Bethlehem).—THE PRESENTATION OF CHRIST IN THE TEMPLE. Luke ii. 22–24 ; compare Haggai ii. 7 and Malachi iii. 1.

SCENE 13.—NICODEMUS' NIGHT WITH JESUS. John ii. 13–16 ; Luke ii. 41–47 ; John iii. 1, 2, and xix. 26, 27.

Zebedee, the father of John the disciple of Jesus, had a house in Jerusalem.

SCENE 14.—Read John iv. 3–6.

Abraham, Gen. xiii. 18 ; *Christ* as Melchizedek, and *Abraham*, Gen. xiv. 18–20 ; *Jacob*, Gen. xxxiii. 18–20 ; *Joseph*, Gen. xxxvii. 12–17, and Joshua xxiv. 32 ; *Joshua*, viii. 30–35, compare Deut. xxvii. 11–15 ; *Woman of Samaria*, John iv. 7–15.

SCENE 15.—THE SEA OF GALILEE, CAPERNAUM, AND CHRIST STILL-ING THE STORM. Mark ii. 1, 2, and iv. 1, 2, 34–41.

He *rebukes* the *winds*, but quiets the frightened sea.

The idea of Demons causing the tempests is expressed in a mosaic over one of the principal entrances of St. Peter's in Rome, executed in 1298. It represents a ship with the disciples. The winds, personified as demons, storm against it. Christ stands on the ship in an attitude of command.

SCENE 16.—THE WALK TO EMMAUS. Luke xxiv. 13–33.

SCENE 17.—Read John xxi. 1–12.

SCENE 18 (Tower of Antonia).—PETER'S RELEASE FROM PRISON. Acts xii. 1–12, 17.

It is a tradition of the Early Church that through all Peter's after-life, from the night he denied his Lord, he rose every morning at the same hour, to pray for renewed forgiveness.

SCENE 19.—THE CONVERSION OF ST. PAUL. Acts ix. 1–8.

SCENE 20.—THE CITY OF PHILIPPI.
Timothy, Luke, Silas, Paul their Leader.

SCENE 21.—PAUL AT TROAS. Acts xx. 6–14.

SCENE 22.—PAUL A PRISONER, ON THE LAST STAGE OF HIS FIRST
JOURNEY TO ROME. Acts xxviii. 13–15, 28, 31.

SCENE 23.—THE MAMERTINE PRISON IN ROME, THE DAY OF PAUL'S
MARTYRDOM. 2 Timothy iv. 6–8.
2 Tim. iv. 16, 17 ; *Onesiphorus,* 2 Tim. i. 16; *Luke,* 2 Tim. iv. 11 ;
Timothy, 2 Tim. iv. 9, 21 ; *Linus,* 2 Tim. iv. 21 ; *Pudens* and his wife
Claudia, 2 Tim. iv. 21.